ELEPHANTS

Please visit our web site at: **www.garethstevens.com**
For a free color catalog describing Gareth Stevens Publishing's
list of high-quality books and multimedia programs, call
1-800-542-2595 (USA) or 1-800-387-3178 (Canada).
Gareth Stevens Publishing's fax: (414) 332-3567.

Library of Congress Cataloging-in-Publication Data

All about elephants.
    Elephants.
        p. cm. — (All about wild animals)
    Previously published in Great Britain as: All about elephants. 2001.
    ISBN 0-8368-4183-2 (lib. bdg.)
        1. Elephants—Juvenile literature. I. Title. II. Series.
    QL737.P98A45 2004
    599.67—dc22   2004040819

This edition first published in 2005 by
Gareth Stevens Publishing
A World Almanac Education Group Company
330 West Olive Street, Suite 100
Milwaukee, Wisconsin 53212 USA

This U.S. edition copyright © 2005 by Gareth Stevens, Inc. Original edition
copyright © 2001 by DeAgostini UK Limited. First published in 2001 as
My Animal Kingdom: All About Elephants by DeAgostini UK Ltd., Griffin House,
161 Hammersmith Road, London W6 8SD, England. Additional end matter
copyright © 2005 by Gareth Stevens, Inc.

Editorial and design: Tucker Slingsby Ltd., London
Gareth Stevens series editor: Catherine Gardner
Gareth Stevens art direction: Tammy West

Picture Credits
Bruce Coleman Collection — M. P. L. Fogden: 27 top.
Digital Vision — 24, 25.
Tony Stone Images — Renee Lynn: 6–7, 11, 26; Manoj Shah: 11, 20; Nicholas
    Parfitt: 15 top; Tim Davies: 16, 17; Jeanne Drake: 17 bottom left; J. Sneesby
    and B. Wilkins: 18, 19 top; Daryl Balfour: 19; Chad Ehlers: 21 top; Pascal
    Crapet: 21 bottom; John Callahan: 22-23; Andrea Booher: 23; Chris
    Simpson: 28; Stuart Westmorland: 27; Hilarie Kavanagh: 29.

Printed in the United States of America

1 2 3 4 5 6 7 8 9 08 07 06 05 04

ALL about WiLD ANiMaLS

ELEPHANTS

Gareth Stevens Publishing
A WORLD ALMANAC EDUCATION GROUP COMPANY

Elephant Facts

Animal group: mammal

Color: gray or brown

Size: Adult males are up to 13 feet (4 meters) tall. Females are up to 8 feet (2.5 m). An adult male is about 23 feet (7 m) long — not including trunk and tail!

Tusk length: up to 10 feet (3 m)

Weight: averages 6 tons

Speed: up to 25 miles (40 kilometers) per hour, but usually from 2.5 to 4 miles (4 to 6 km) per hour, or about the same speed as people walk

Eats: grass, roots, bark, shoots, leaves, and fruit

Drinks: about 22 gallons (83 liters) each day

Lives: up to 30 years in the wild and up to 80 years in captivity

CONTENTS

A Closer Look 6

Home, Sweet Home 10

Neighbors 12

The Family 14

Life in the Hot Sun 18

Favorite Foods 20

Danger! 22

An Elephant's Day .24

Relatives 26

Humans and Elephants 28

Glossary 30

Index 32

Words that appear in the glossary
are printed in **boldface** type the
first time they occur in the text.

A Closer Look

Elephants are huge! They are the biggest land animals alive today. Male African elephants weigh as much as 17,000 pounds (7,700 kilograms), which is about the same as the weight of two hundred children. Elephants grow up to 13 feet (4 meters) tall — the height of an adult person standing on another person's shoulders. To get enough energy for their huge bodies, elephants spend most of the day looking for food.

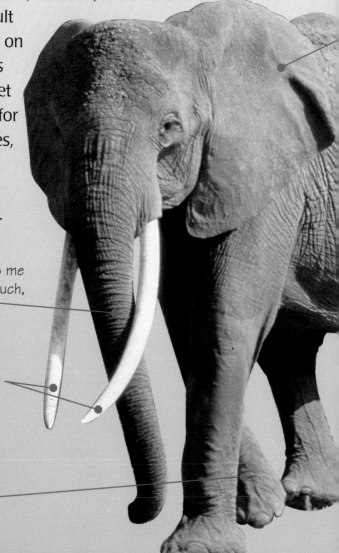

My long trunk helps me eat, drink, smell, touch, and shower!

I use my long tusks to tear bark off of trees and dig up tasty roots.

I have strong, muscular legs.

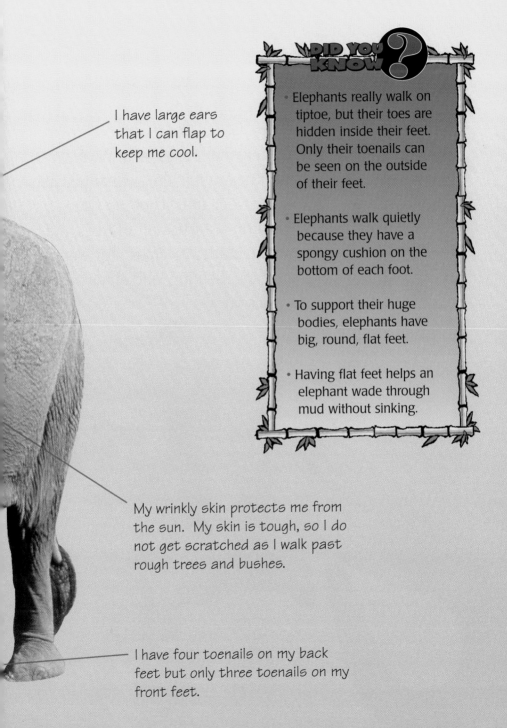

I have large ears that I can flap to keep me cool.

DID YOU KNOW ?

• Elephants really walk on tiptoe, but their toes are hidden inside their feet. Only their toenails can be seen on the outside of their feet.

• Elephants walk quietly because they have a spongy cushion on the bottom of each foot.

• To support their huge bodies, elephants have big, round, flat feet.

• Having flat feet helps an elephant wade through mud without sinking.

My wrinkly skin protects me from the sun. My skin is tough, so I do not get scratched as I walk past rough trees and bushes.

I have four toenails on my back feet but only three toenails on my front feet.

An elephant has a large head and the biggest brain of any animal on land. Its brain is four times bigger than a human brain! An elephant also has big ears and a long trunk. The elephant's big, flexible trunk is a very special piece of equipment. A trunk works like a nose, a top lip, and a hand all in one. An elephant uses its trunk to smell, touch, and hold things. With its trunk, an elephant is able to scratch its ear, throw an object, and scoop up water. A trunk is strong enough to rip branches off of trees, but it is gentle enough to pull up blades of grass. An elephant relies on its senses of touching, hearing, and smelling more than on its sense of vision.

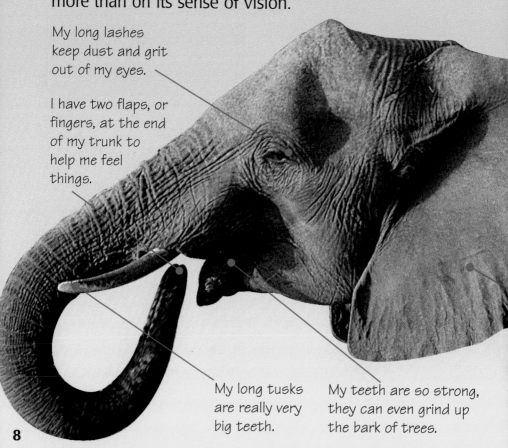

My long lashes keep dust and grit out of my eyes.

I have two flaps, or fingers, at the end of my trunk to help me feel things.

My long tusks are really very big teeth.

My teeth are so strong, they can even grind up the bark of trees.

African elephants have two types of teeth. They have long tusks, which are really incisors, the type of teeth used for tearing. Elephants also have huge molars, which are the type of teeth used for chewing. The molars wear down fast, so new molars grow behind the old molars and push out the worn teeth.

Adult elephants have two tusks that are made of ivory.

Molars are replaced up to five times in an elephant's life.

HEAD TO HEAD

The two main types of elephants are African elephants and Asian elephants. At first, all elephants may look the same, but it is easy to see differences between African and Asian types of elephants.

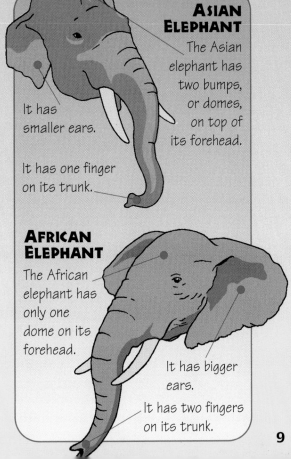

ASIAN ELEPHANT

The Asian elephant has two bumps, or domes, on top of its forehead.

It has smaller ears.

It has one finger on its trunk.

AFRICAN ELEPHANT

The African elephant has only one dome on its forehead.

It has bigger ears.

It has two fingers on its trunk.

My ears are big and wide. With my excellent hearing, I listen for other elephants when they trumpet, blow, puff, or rumble to me.

HOME, SWEET HOME

Asian elephants live in India and in parts of southeastern Asia. They live in areas that have large forests. African elephants live in most parts of Africa except the desert. African elephants live in areas of savanna or bushland. A savanna is a wide area of grassy, flat land. On a savanna, the weather is warm all year. Bushland is like a savanna, but it has more trees and bushes, and the land is not quite as flat. Some African elephants live at the edges of forests, where the shade gives some relief from the hot weather, but most elephants prefer to roam on a savanna.

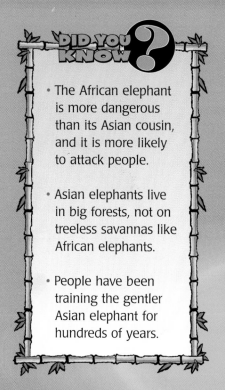

DID YOU KNOW?

• The African elephant is more dangerous than its Asian cousin, and it is more likely to attack people.

• Asian elephants live in big forests, not on treeless savannas like African elephants.

• People have been training the gentler Asian elephant for hundreds of years.

WHERE IN THE WORLD?

Although African elephants and Asian elephants live on different continents, they have the same problem — finding space to live. Elephants need a lot of room to roam and to eat, but they keep losing land to people who build houses and cities. When people take land, they spoil the habitat, or the natural conditions, that elephants need to survive.

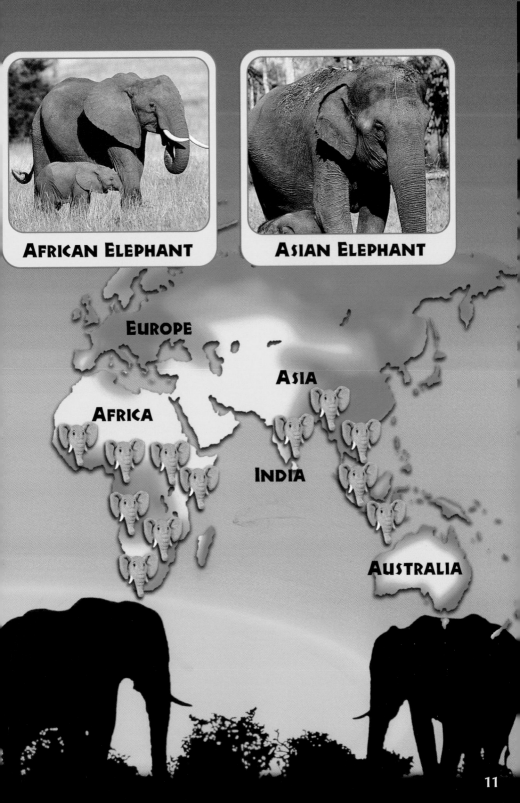

AFRICAN ELEPHANT

ASIAN ELEPHANT

EUROPE

ASIA

AFRICA

INDIA

AUSTRALIA

NEIGHBORS

African elephants share savanna and bushland areas with plant-eating animals such as **antelopes**, meat-eating animals such as lions, and many kinds of birds, insects, and **reptiles**. Elephants are very good neighbors. When elephants eat, they tear down branches and scatter leaves that smaller animals can eat. They dig up mud to protect their skin, which makes bigger water holes for all animals to use. Even an elephant's **dung** improves the habitat by spreading seeds and fertilizing the soil.

ONE BIG NEIGHBOR

Another big African animal is a hippopotamus. A hippo lives on a savanna and eats plants, but it does not compete with an elephant for land or food. A hippo spends its days in a river or lake and eats the grassy types of plants that grow near water.

HOW ARE ELEPHANTS HELPFUL?

BIRDS

Cattle egrets and other birds eat the insects that elephants disturb as they walk through long grass.

CREEPY-CRAWLIES

Beetles, flies, worms, and other creatures feed on elephant dung! They help put **nutrients** back into the soil.

PEOPLE

People often follow paths trampled by elephants. Elephant paths are an easy way to get through the grass and shrubs on a savanna or bushland.

PLANTS

Many seeds remain whole as they pass through the stomach of an elephant. Then they grow in its dung!

KEEP CLEAR

Some dangerous animals live in the same parts of Africa as elephants. A leopard (*top*) hides on a branch until it sees small animals to hunt. Lions, which are bigger than leopards and hunt in groups, do not attack healthy adult elephants. Even an African buffalo (*bottom*), a fierce animal with big horns, stays away from elephants.

THE FAMILY

Elephants live together in large family groups, or herds, of about twenty elephants. All of the elephants in the herd are related to each other. Mothers and their sisters, along with all of their daughters and young sons, live together in a herd. Adult males, called bulls, usually live alone or in **bachelor** groups. A bull remains close to its herd so it can fight any bull elephants that try to take over the herd. A young elephant, called a calf, stays with its mother, and all females help take care of the younger calves. When a male elephant is able to live on its own, its father chases it away from the herd so it can start its own family.

Elephant calves depend on their mothers for protection and food for several years. The calves do not need to find their own food, so they have lots of time to play. Playing is really a way of getting ready for adult life. Young bull elephants play-fight with each other. Their friendly fights help them practice for the future when they need to fight other bulls to protect themselves and their herds. Young females help the mothers take care of the youngest calves in the herd.

LEADING LADY

One female elephant always is in charge of each herd. She is called the **matriarch** and is usually one of the oldest females in the herd. She is experienced and wise and decides when and where it is safe for the herd to eat and drink.

Baby File

Birth

An adult female elephant, called a cow, most often gives birth to a single calf. Twins are rarely born. Other females help the mother and her newborn calf and scare away any enemies. The calf can stand on its own legs within an hour after it is born, but it cannot control its trunk for about four months. Using a trunk takes strength and plenty of practice.

Up to Four Years Old

Young elephants have lots to learn. They depend on their mothers and other members of the herd to take good care of them. Older elephants can chase off **predators** and pull calves out of the mud if they get stuck. Calves drink milk from their mothers until they are about four years old.

More Than Five Years Old

When a young bull is about five years old, it is chased away from its mother's herd. It is not full grown yet, but it can take care of itself.

Big Feet

The world must look like a forest of gray legs to a young elephant. It needs to be careful not to get underfoot! When danger lurks, a little elephant finds a safe hiding spot under those long adult legs.

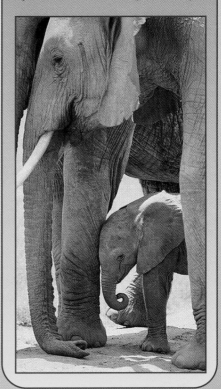

LIFE IN THE HOT SUN

Staying cool in the hot African sun isn't easy for animals as big as elephants. To beat the heat, elephants try lots of different tricks, and they have plenty of fun while they cool off! When elephants are very hot, they head to the nearest lake or water hole and take a shower. Elephants use their trunks like hoses to squirt water over themselves or each other. It takes practice, but an elephant can squirt water all over its own body.

THE COLOR OF MUD

Elephants use mud and dust to protect their skin from the scorching sun. They spend so much time covered in mud and dust that the color of their skin looks like the color of the local mud! Red, black, and even yellow elephants have been spotted walking away from mud baths.

MUD, GLORIOUS MUD!

One good way for elephants to escape the heat is to take a mud bath. They cover their skin with sticky mud, which feels cool and refreshing. They don't bother to rinse after a mud bath! The mud dries on their skin and protects it from the burning rays of the sun.

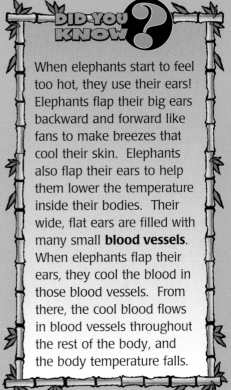

DUST OFF!

Even elephants can get a sunburn. Their home on the savanna has few trees that provide shade and an escape from the sun's burning rays. To help prevent sunburn, elephants cover their backs with dust. The dusting has another benefit. It helps keep biting insects away.

FAVORITE FOODS

Elephants have big appetites. An elephant can eat up to 440 pounds (200 kg) of food a day, or about as much as the total weight of three grown humans! It is no wonder elephants must spend up to eighteen hours a day eating. They eat mainly grass, but they also eat bark, roots, fruits, twigs, and leaves. Some of their favorite foods are green grass, **shoots**, and the buds of trees and shrubs that grow during the rainy season. During the dry season, the grass dies. Then elephants eat more from trees and bushes. To find enough food, a herd needs a lot of land.

SALTY TASTE

All animals need to eat some salt. Animals that eat only plants, such as elephants, do not get salt from their food. Elephants eat the salt they find in the soil. A place that has especially salty soil or rock is called a salt lick. Asian elephants (*bottom*) enjoy a salty snack!

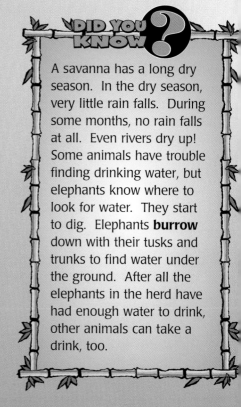

DID YOU KNOW?

A savanna has a long dry season. In the dry season, very little rain falls. During some months, no rain falls at all. Even rivers dry up! Some animals have trouble finding drinking water, but elephants know where to look for water. They start to dig. Elephants **burrow** down with their tusks and trunks to find water under the ground. After all the elephants in the herd have had enough water to drink, other animals can take a drink, too.

FINDING FOOD

Foraging takes up many hours of an elephant's day. Elephants that live on a savanna look for the greenest grass for most of their meals. Elephants that live closer to forests may not have as much grass to eat, but they choose their meals from many other kinds of plants and trees.

TREETOP TREATS!

Trunks are very useful for reaching the tasty treats that grow in the treetops! Elephants stretch their trunks to pick sweet fruit and berries. Bananas are a favorite treat.

DANGER!

Elephants have no animal enemies. Life can be tough on the savanna, though. Like other animals, elephants are in danger from starvation and **drought** during the dry season. They can become sick or injured, too. An injured elephant may not be able to walk to food and water. The other elephants in the herd always try to take care of a sick elephant by supporting it when it tries to stand.

DID YOU KNOW?

When an elephant dies, other members of the herd may bury the body by covering it with long grass, branches, and soil. If elephants see another elephant's skeleton, they may sniff at the remains, remove the tusks, and scatter the bones. When elephants walk near the place where a member of the herd died in the past, they may pause. Perhaps elephants are able to remember their dead relatives.

Ivory Hunters

Elephant tusks are made of a hard, creamy white material called ivory. At one time, people collected lots of ivory and carved it into delicate ornaments and beautiful jewelry. Ivory was so valuable that people killed thousands of elephants just for their tusks. Now, most African countries do not allow elephant hunting. Some people, known as **poachers**, illegally kill elephants and sell the ivory tusks for large amounts of money.

Thirsty Work!

Elephants sometimes walk long distances to find enough food and water for the entire herd.

23

An Elephant's Day

It was still dark when we woke, but we elephants never sleep for long periods of time. We do take naps.

5:00 AM

Other animals woke up as the sun rose. I just kept on eating. It's the rainy season, so there's plenty of grass to eat.

6:00 AM

My calf spent most of her day playing. She kept trying to catch my tail with her trunk! It is just a game to her, but this game helps her learn to control her long trunk.

8:00 AM

We headed for a water hole. It was time for a cool drink and a dip.

10:00 AM

To beat the noon heat, I plastered some cool mud on my back and settled down for a nap. My calf stretched out in my shadow.

12 NOON

The matriarch of our herd, who happens to be my aunt, led us in search of more food.

3:00 PM

We passed by another herd. I hadn't seen some of those elephants for years!

4:00 PM

We saw some humans. These days, most humans carry cameras, not guns. We stayed away anyway. Humans are noisy, and they can be dangerous.

5:00 PM

6:00 PM As the sun set, we walked back to the water hole. The calves practiced squirting water on their backs. They managed to get all of the mothers wet, too!

7:00 PM Darkness fell, but that didn't keep us away from our meal. Elephants usually find food by smell and touch.

9:00 PM I found a fantastic tree — perfect for a good back rub. It felt great to scratch off the caked-on mud and little insects that irritated my skin.

11:30 PM Cool nighttime is the best time for eating. Sometimes while we eat, one elephant reaches out a trunk to another just to say hello.

1:00 AM After eating, it's time to sleep. It won't be long before the day starts again, and I usually wake up hungry!

RELATIVES

The African elephant and the Asian elephant are the only two kinds of elephants alive today. Their closest relatives in the animal world are hyraxes, manatees, and dugongs. Hyraxes are furry animals that live in Africa. They make almost as much noise as elephants, but they are smaller and look more like rabbits. Manatees and dugongs are big — they weigh as much as 2,535 pounds (1,150 kg). They eat the plants that grow in the water where they live. Manatees and dugongs look like seals and have wide tails that help them swim.

WOOLLY MAMMOTHS

One relative of elephants, a giant beast called a woolly mammoth, has become **extinct.** More than forty thousand years ago, woolly mammoths lived in cold parts of the world. They were even bigger than today's elephants, but they had many of the same features. Their tusks grew up to 16 feet (5 meters) long — longer than a car! Unlike an elephant, the woolly mammoth had long, shaggy hair to keep its body warm.

BIG NOSE!

The elephant seal gets its name because of its huge nose, but it is no relation to true elephants at all!

MERMAID MYSTERY

Dugongs and manatees are strange-looking animals that live in the water. Some people believe that stories of imaginary sea creatures called mermaids began when sailors saw dugongs in the water. The stream-lined shape of a dugong may have seemed to have the upper body of a human and the tail of a fish.

DID YOU KNOW?

Animals that have long or big noses are often given names that include the word "elephant." For example, the elephant shrew is a tiny animal that has a long, pointed nose. One kind of fish is called the elephant-snout fish!

HUMANS AND ELEPHANTS

Elephants are well-known animals. They are considered gentle, wise creatures. People are fascinated by their size and strength. In some countries, people worship elephants. In India, the head of the god Ganesha looks like an elephant. Other people believe that touching an elephant can help them tell right from wrong. On special occasions, people in parts of Asia decorate elephants with jewels and paint them bright colors.

WORKING ELEPHANTS

In Asia, people train elephants to move logs. Elephants can carry small logs in their trunks and push larger ones along on the ground. In some places, elephants are trained to carry people or heavy loads or to perform circus tricks. Many people think that elephant training can be cruel and that **captive** elephants do not receive good care.

WILD ELEPHANTS

The remaining wild African elephants need to live in **game reserves** and national parks. As the human population grows, wild elephants are pushed into smaller and smaller areas. In the national parks and game reserves, people can better protect elephants from poachers.

DID YOU KNOW?

- The word *elephantine* means "huge" or "clumsy." It's true that elephants are large, but for their size, they really are very **nimble**.

- The word *elephant* describes a sheet of paper of a certain size — a very big size. One sheet measures 28 inches (71 centimeters) wide.

- Jumbo was the name of the first elephant that appeared at the London Zoo. Today, we call any extra-large thing, such as a jet, jumbo.

ELEPHANTS AT WAR

In the past, elephants were used in war. Soldiers rode into battle on the backs of elephants dressed in armor. Facing a herd of such mighty animals must have been a scary sight for any soldier on the other side! More than two thousand years ago, a soldier named Hannibal led 40,000 men and 38 elephants from Carthage in North Africa to Italy to attack the Romans. Men and elephants traveled through Spain and across the French Alps. The army may even have used rafts to move the elephants across the Rhone River!

GLOSSARY

ANTELOPES
Animals that look like deer but have long horns without any branches. They live in Africa and parts of Asia and are known for their fast running speed.

BACHELOR
A male animal that does not have a mate.

BLOOD VESSELS
Narrow tubes that allow blood to flow throughout the body.

BURROW
To dig a tunnel or hole in the ground.

CAPTIVE
Kept in a place with no chance to leave.

DROUGHT
A long period of very dry weather.

DUNG
The solid waste produced by an animal; manure.

EXTINCT
Having all of the members of a certain kind of animal or plant dead; having no more of that kind left alive.

FORAGING
Searching for food.

GAME RESERVES
Areas of land set aside as places where wild animals can live and where hunting and human settlements are restricted.

IVORY
A hard, creamy white substance that makes up the tusks of animals such as elephants, walruses, and hippos. People use it to carve decorative objects. Some people believe it has magical properties.

MATRIARCH
A female who is the head of a family group. The matriarch of an elephant herd decides when the herd should move to a new territory and where it should go.

NIMBLE
Able to move easily and quickly.

NUTRIENTS
The parts of food needed by humans, animals, and plants to stay healthy.

PREDATORS
Animals that hunt other animals for food.

POACHERS
People who hunt and kill animals illegally.

REPTILES
Cold-blooded animals that have backbones, crawl or walk on short legs, and produce their young by laying eggs.

SHOOTS
Young plants that have just grown above the soil or the new parts that are beginning to develop on a plant that already exists.

INDEX

African buffalo 13
African elephants 6, 9, 10, 11, 12, 26, 28
Asian elephants 9, 10, 11, 26

bulls 14, 16, 17
bushland 10, 12, 13

calves 14, 16, 17, 24, 25
cows 17

drinking 6, 16, 17, 20, 24
dugongs 27
dung 12, 13

ears 7, 8, 9, 19
eyes 8

feet 7, 17
fighting 14, 16
food 6, 12, 16, 20, 21, 22, 23, 24, 25
forests 10, 21

habitats 10, 12
heads 8, 9, 28
herds 14, 16, 17, 20, 22, 23, 24, 29
hippos 12

insects 12, 13, 19, 25
ivory 9, 23

legs 6, 17
leopards 13

manatees 27
matriarchs 16, 24

rainy season 20, 24

salt 20
savanna 10, 12, 13, 19, 20, 21, 22
skin 7, 12, 18, 19, 25

teeth 8, 9
toes 7
training 10, 28
trunks 6, 8, 9, 17, 18, 20, 21, 24, 25
tusks 6, 8, 9, 20, 22, 23, 26

walking 7, 13, 22, 23, 25
water 8, 18, 20, 22, 23, 25, 26, 27
water holes 12, 24, 25
weight 6
woolly mammoths 26